Three Minutes With God
A WEEKLY DEVOTIONAL FOR INSPIRATION AND ENCOURAGEMENT

Jarvis E. Bailey

authorHOUSE®

AuthorHouse™
1663 Liberty Drive, Suite 200
Bloomington, IN 47403
www.authorhouse.com
Phone: 1-800-839-8640

© *2008 Jarvis E. Bailey. All rights reserved.*

No part of this book may be reproduced, stored in a retrieval system, or transmitted by any means without the written permission of the author.

First published by AuthorHouse 11/19/2008

ISBN: 978-1-4389-2496-0 (sc)
ISBN: 978-1-4389-2497-7 (hc)

Library of Congress Control Number: 2008910748

Printed in the United States of America
Bloomington, Indiana

This book is printed on acid-free paper.

To God Be the Glory

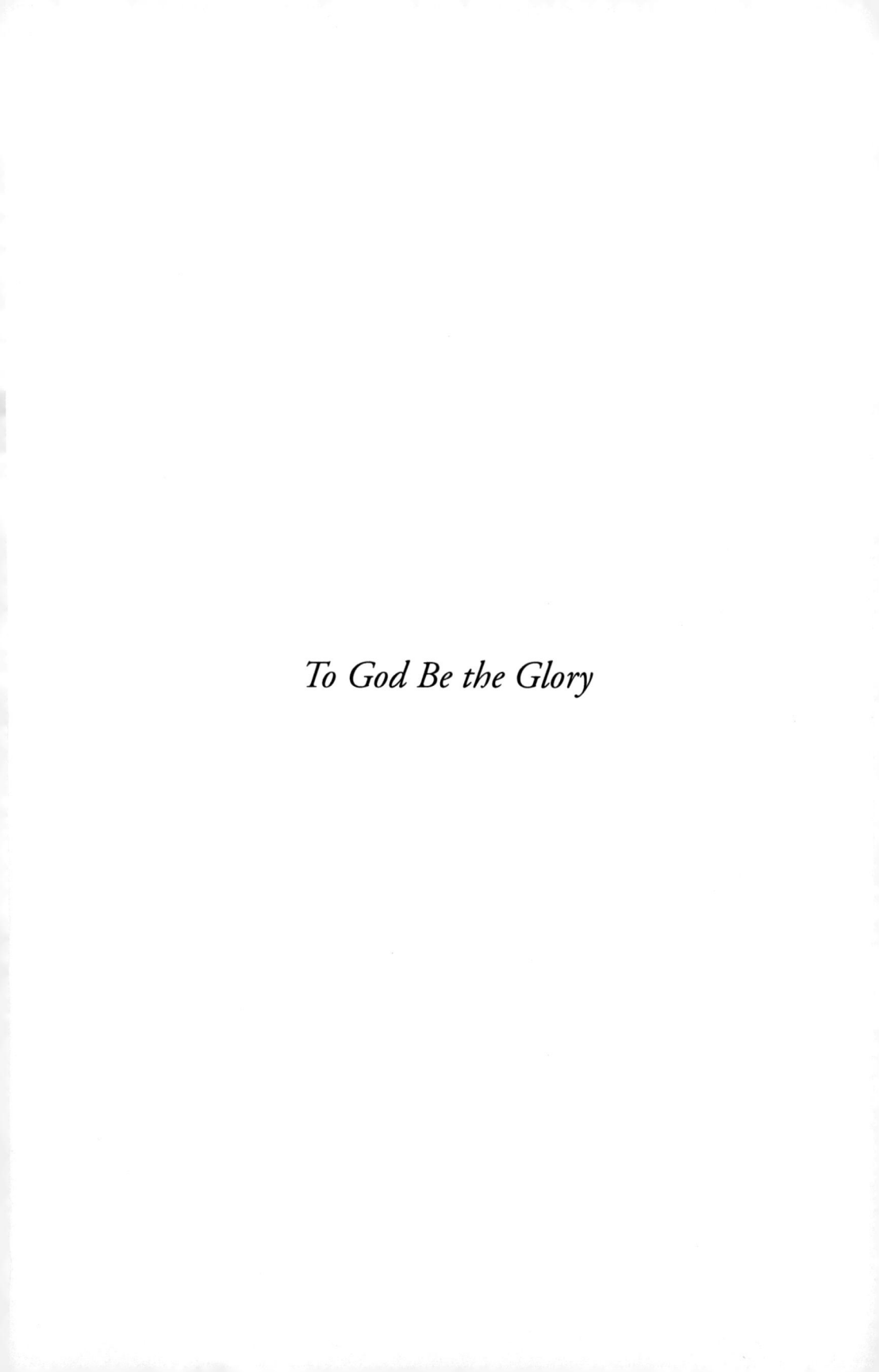

The Greatest Commandment Campaign

One of the teachers of the law came and heard them debating. Noticing that Jesus had given them a good answer, he asked him, "Of all the commandments, which is the most important?" "The most important one" answered Jesus, "is this: 'Hear, O Israel, the Lord our God, the Lord is one. Love the Lord your God with all your heart and with all your soul and with all your mind and with all your strength.' The second is this: 'Love your neighbor as yourself.' There is no commandment greater than these." (NIV, Mark 12:28-31)

In response to *The Greatest Commandment*, ninety percent of book sale profits will be donated to causes that enrich the lives of others. For more information visit:

www.jarvisbailey.com

What's Inside

What I'm Learning

Why *Three Minutes with God*

Weekly Devotionals

Acknowledgments

Notes

WHAT I'M LEARNING

The Importance of Devotional Time

I am at an age and a place in life where I make every attempt to maximize my efforts. I've wasted enough time, so I want to spend what's left doing only the things that matter most. So believe me when I say that devotional time is important.

Over the years, I have observed that the most fulfilling part of my day is time spent with God. The spiritual necessities required for me to meet the challenges of the day are born and nurtured during my time alone with God. My devotional time is a wellspring of hope, courage, peace, and joy.

I'm convinced that the quality of my life depends on the quality of my relationship with God, and that spending time in the presence of God is critical to my existence. In fact, I believe that loving God "with all your heart and with all your soul and with all your mind and with all your strength" (Mark 12:30, NKJV) is the most important aspect of a person's life.

As you read this book, please know that I have made every attempt to create a work that is meaningful and relevant, and that will stand the test of time. I pray that through these words you will not only feel the beat of my heart, but more importantly, you will feel and know the heart of God.

Why *Three Minutes With God*

I have often tried to keep up with the demands of a daily devotional, but by the second week I've usually fallen behind. That's when the frustration sets in. Now I'm playing catch-up and reading out of obligation, not for reflection. By the third week I'm most likely done, with the expectation that I'll try it again at some other time—maybe in another year.

I wrote this book for people like me—people with too many things to do and not enough time to do them. While anyone can enjoy the book, it will be especially helpful to those who are not always able to make time for devotions, but realize the value it adds to their lives.

The idea was to create a resource that was practical and easy to use—a devotional book that people would look forward to reading. I wanted busy people like me not to feel burdened by another task, but excited about a new opportunity—an opportunity to slow down for a moment with God, or just three minutes, to be exact.

The methodology is simple: read, reflect, and respond. The scripture and the devotion are the same for the entire week. Each devotion provides an opportunity for journaling and praying, as well as a call to action. So, if you miss a day, don't stress. The material is the same as the day before, and it'll be the same for the next day. The goal is for you to personalize and enjoy your devotional time. How you spend your three minutes with God is up to you. My prayer is that you do spend the time with God. After all, it's only three minutes!

Contents

1. A Word of Encouragement 2
2. Man Up! 6
3. Real Security 10
4. Be King for a Day 14
5. You Can Run, But You Can't Hide 18
6. Who Knows? 22
7. I Surrender All 26
8. Thirty Seconds to Fame 30
9. It's How You Finish 34
10. Coffee-Bean Women 38
11. What's in a Name? 42
12. God Willing 46
13. Finish the Race 50
14. More Than Enough 54
15. A Work in Progress 58
16. Unity Is Power 62
17. Pray for Peace 66
18. A Different Way 70
19. My Inheritance 74
20. Chickens Can't Fly 78
21. The Old Landmark 82
22. Meritorious Service 86
23. A Sure Foundation 90
24. Those Crazy Christians 94
25. Authentic Manhood 98
26. It Ain't Always About Us 102
27. Teach Us to Pray 106
28. The Real World 110
29. Ready for Community? 114
30. Beginning at the End 118
31. By Our Love 122
32. It's Your Availability 126
33. Do It! 130
34. Amazing Faith! 134
35. Cash versus Character 138

36. Where's the Fruit?	142
37. Hard Work	146
38. The Children Are Our Future	150
39. Good Examples	154
40. Keep the Faith, Baby	158
41. A New Thing?	162
42. I Pray For You	166
43. Come	170
44. The Secret of Success	174
45. A Lesson in Giving	178
46. The Right Question	182
47. Remember Who You Are	186
48. Give Thanks	190
49. Moral Discourse	194
50. Impossible Is Nothing	198
51. Do You See Divinity?	202
52. Grace and Peace	206
Acknowledgments	209
Notes	211

Week One

A Word of Encouragement

For I am persuaded that neither death nor life, nor angels nor principalities nor powers, nor things present nor things to come, nor height nor depth, nor any other created thing, shall be able to separate us from the love of God which is in Christ Jesus our Lord.
—Romans 8:38–39

Regardless of who you are, where you live, or what you do, there are times in your life when you need to be encouraged. Life has lots of ups and downs—and when it's down, we need someone or something to cheer our hearts and lift up our spirits. Maybe one of those times is right now. (If not, as my mother always says, "Keep on living—your day is coming.") Just know that every now and then, we all need a word of encouragement.

The apostle Paul understood this well. He instructs us that "there is now no condemnation to them which are in Christ Jesus," and that "all things work together for good to them that love God, to them who are called according to His purpose." Paul knew, as we should know, that "if God is for us, who can be against us?"

As the issues of life persist, and as the adversary tries to use the weapon of discouragement against us, may we be encouraged by the reassurance that God still loves us and cares for us—and may we know with the utmost confidence that He is still in charge. And even though we are sometimes shaky in our relationships with Christ, the good news is that nothing can separate Christ from us. Now that's tough love. Be strong and be of good courage, and may God always reign supreme in your life. Grace and peace …

—Jarvis

Reflect ...
What is God saying to me?

God wants us to be (bear) the likeness of Christ so that we can be firstborn. In other words, our Christlikeness will bring birth to others.

We are conquerors in the midst of hardship, danger, famine.

Respond ...
In response to the devotional, how can I reflect Jesus in my actions?

- Look to Jesus in every action. Keep my eyes focused. Ask for wisdom. Ask to have my eyes "other" oriented, not "self" oriented.

This week I will ...

- Cont. to Trust in the Lord and look to Him. My emotions are a very bad plumb line.
- Ask God to teach me to be "other" centered
-

How is the Holy Spirit leading me to pray?

I have been through a lot of downs this year. I will cont. to pray the Scriptures like I have been. Pray God will teach me to be "other" centered.

Week Two

Man Up!

"And if it seems evil unto you to serve the Lord, choose you this day whom ye will serve ... But as for me and my house, we will serve the Lord."

—Joshua 24:15

I've always thought of myself as a *cool dude*. But my wife quickly brings me back to reality by reminding me of the eleventh commandment: "Thou shalt not deceive thyself." In my attempt to be cool, my children have taught me a new saying: "Man up." I am told that "man up" is a directive or a challenge for a person to make a decision to act. If Joshua lived in our time, and was cool like me, he would say to his listeners, "Man up!"

Most of us have heard the *life-is-about-choices* speech. And we all have been told at least once, "You are in life where you choose to be." For sure, there are lots of choices in life, and we don't always make good ones. And while I believe that sometimes there are circumstances that supersede our ability to choose, when it comes to serving and loving God, the choice is *always* ours.

I think that Joshua was right in asking the Israelites to man up. But first he reminded them of their relationship with God. Maybe that would help us, too. Maybe it would help if we remembered, as the Psalm declares, that "the Lord *is* good; His mercy *is* everlasting, and His truth *endures* to all generations."

"Choose you this day whom ye will serve." Remember, you get to decide. The power is all yours. Whose side are you on? Man up!

—Jarvis

Reflect …
What is God saying to me?

You are unable to serve Me without My help. But you must consciously choose to serve me minute by minute. Then I will be with you and enable you.

Respond …
In response to the devotional, how can I reflect Jesus in my actions?

- Choose to stay in the Word
- Choose to stay connected
- Don't let other things impede your relationship with Christ.
- Seek to be "other" minded.

This week I will …

-
-
-

How is the Holy Spirit leading me to pray?

Week Three

REAL SECURITY

Some trust in chariots and some in horses, but we trust in the name of the LORD our God.
—Psalm 20:7

When a radio station recently reported that a certain celebrity received a $260 million paycheck, I was amazed. "That's ridiculous," I thought. But I quickly realized that *my* paycheck and *my* lifestyle were ridiculous, too. It just depended on who was doing the judging. And I had to admit that I liked my lifestyle. I liked living the "American Dream" and being free to pursue my heart's desires.

That same day I heard a politician state that he would never use nuclear weapons to fight terrorism. I respected his view, but I wasn't sure I agreed. Again, I liked my way of life. And while I touted myself as a man of peace, I liked having the biggest stick at the table. I liked my job, my house, and my cars. I liked living in America. And I didn't take kindly to the idea of giving it all up.

Was I finding some comfort, even some security, in all my possessions, and especially in my nationality? Then I was reminded of David's words to his warriors as they prepared for battle: "Some trust in chariots and some in horses, but we trust in the name of the LORD our God."

Growing up, I learned a song that repeated the phrase, "I will trust in the Lord till I die!" In our superficial world, may that song become a repeated theme in our lives as we seek to honor the source of our *real* security.

—**Jarvis**

Reflect …
What is God saying to me?

My biggest downfall is in not trusting in the Lord. I haven't thanked Him even in the hard times because I had been trusting in other things and they failed me. I have made many bad decisions based on insecurity.

Respond …
In response to the devotional, how can I reflect Jesus in my actions?

I must begin to pray more and take risks. I live to confined in my secure nest.

This week I will …

- *Ask God to help me to become a prayer warrior*
- *Ask God to make it clear when I need to step outside my comfort zone.*
- *Relax in the Lord and trust Him.*

How is the Holy Spirit leading me to pray?

Holy Spirit, how do I live my Christian life and ideals when I do not have the support in my home?

Week Four

BE KING FOR A DAY

Only take heed to yourself, and diligently keep yourself, lest you forget the things your eyes have seen, and lest they depart from your heart all the days of your life. And teach them to your children and your grandchildren.
—Deuteronomy 4:9

Be King for a day—lest we forget! What better way to commemorate Martin Luther King than by living his dream: a dream for a better world; a dream of hope, of peace, and of love; a dream inclusive of all humankind; a dream to which he dedicated his life.

Be King for a day! Let your light so shine, as Dr. King's did, that others may see your good works and glorify the Father in heaven. Dr. King's light still shines. The message he brought and the victories he won continue to brighten our lives. Try to love people, as Dr. King did, not because of who they are, but because they are created in the image of God. Dr. King tried to love *everybody*. Maybe he knew that love believes all things, hopes all things, and endures all things.

Be King for a day, and keep the dream alive—until, as Haile Selassie I of Ethiopia proclaimed, "the philosophy that holds one race superior and another inferior is finally and permanently discredited and abandoned ... until there are no longer first class and second class citizens of any nation ... until the basic human rights are equally guaranteed to all without regards to race."[1] Keep the dream alive.

MLK gave his life away ... and it was not in vain. Keep the dream alive. Be King for a day—lest we forget.

—**Jarvis**

Reflect …
What is God saying to me?

Eph. 6:4 - Fathers, do not exasperate your children. Bring them up in training/inst. of the Lord.

Do not allow idols to come into your lives. (Think on Daniel - Babylon - I am and there is no one besides me)

Respond …
In response to the devotional, how can I reflect Jesus in my actions?

Become "tuned in"/discerning

This week I will …

-

-

-

How is the Holy Spirit leading me to pray?

Week Five

You Can Run, But You Can't Hide

The eyes of the Lord are in every place, keeping watch on the evil and the good.
—*Proverbs 15:3*

It was 1946, and the rematch between Joe Louis, the "Brown Bomber," and Billy Conn, the "Pittsburg Kid," was set. In the first fight, Conn almost defeated the world heavyweight champion by outmaneuvering him with a "hit-and-run" boxing style. When asked about Conn's style for the rematch, Louis, who was known as a great puncher, replied: "He can run, but he can't hide."

There are times when running seems like the right thing to do. And in some situations, it may well be the wise choice. But for many of life's difficult issues, running often is only a temporary solution. "You can run, but you can't hide." If nothing is done to solve the problem, when the running and hiding are over, the problem may still remain.

Solomon's wisdom suggests that God sees everything—that nothing is hidden from God. On one hand, we are challenged to live righteously, knowing that God is always watching. Yet on the other hand, we are comforted by the knowledge that God is never out of reach.

It may have been unsettling for the Pittsburgh Kid to hear the Brown Bomber suggest that there was no place for him to hide. But for us, we can always run to the One who Isaiah claimed "shall be as a hiding place from the wind, and a cover from the storm."

—**Jarvis**

Reflect ...
What is God saying to me?

II Chron 16:9 - God's eyes range through the earth searching for those fully committed to Him.
Job 10:19 - We are not capable of seeing
Heb. 4:13 - Everything is uncovered; nothing hidden

Respond ...
In response to the devotional, how can I reflect Jesus in my actions?

This week I will ...

-

-

-

How is the Holy Spirit leading me to pray?

Week Six

WHO KNOWS?

For if you remain completely silent at this time, relief and deliverance will arise for the Jews from another place ... Yet who knows whether you have come to the kingdom for such a time as this?
—Esther 4:14

In the book of Esther, there is no explicit reference to God. Yet, as the story unfolds, it becomes clear that God is in control. Even Esther appears unaware of God's involvement. But the fact that God is not mentioned, or that God is not recognized, does not mean that God is not at work.

The Greek thinker Socrates believed that asking questions would eventually lead to the truth. Apparently, Socrates wasn't the only one who understood the power of the right question. With the plight of the people at stake, Esther's uncle Mordecai realizes that deliverance is certain because he knows that God has a plan. But he challenges Esther to fulfill her role in that plan by asking her this question: "Who knows?"

Many agree that we are living in a crucial time. There is also agreement that God is still in control. So, if, indeed, "leaders are called into existence by circumstances,"[2] as Leonard Sweet suggests, *who knows whether **you** have come... for such a time as this*?

Esther was crowned queen, and ultimately claimed her esteemed place in history. Who knows? Maybe it's your time to do something extraordinary. Are you feeling challenged to fulfill the plans God has for you? Then here again is the question: *Who knows whether you have come ... for such a time as this*? The answer: God knows. And now you do, too.

—Jarvis

Reflect ...
What is God saying to me?

Not only should you say you trust me. Remember that I have a plan for your life. The events aren't random. There is a purpose in it all. You have been brought to this family for a time such as this. God intended it for good ... the saving of many lives.

Respond ...
In response to the devotional, how can I reflect Jesus in my actions?

Learn to forgive
Stay open
Build intimacy

This week I will ...

-

-

-

How is the Holy Spirit leading me to pray?

Week Seven

I Surrender All

So when Jesus heard these things, He said to him, "You still lack one thing. Sell all that you have and distribute to the poor, and you will have treasure in heaven; and come, follow Me."
—Luke 18:22

I have known a number of people who have spent a great amount of time, including a few sleepless nights, discussing whether or not they had to sell all their *stuff* to be a follower of Jesus. I once heard a very wealthy Christian gentleman give an hour lecture explaining how Jesus could not possibly have been referring to him. But why is this issue so troubling?

For sure, it has something to do with money, possessions, and power. And Jesus certainly knows, and often teaches about, the potential dangers of focusing on worldly treasures. But the man in the story appears to have all the correct answers—he knows the commandments, and he's kept them from his youth. Yet when Jesus tells him that to inherit eternal life he must sell all that he has and give it to the poor, well, that makes him unhappy because he was very rich. How often in our lives have we been unhappy because we've been asked to give up some of our possessions to help someone less fortunate?

Jesus said what needed to be said to a rich young ruler—that was his "hot button." Maybe the possessions you need to sell aren't material at all. Maybe it's an attitude, or your ambitions, or your personal plans for the future—I don't know. But I do know that to truly follow Jesus, we must be willing to surrender all—to give up our stuff for the cause of Christ—so that we can say, "I'm yours, Lord … completely yours."

—Jarvis

Reflect ...
What is God saying to me?

Respond ...
In response to the devotional, how can I reflect Jesus in my actions?

This week I will ...

-
-
-

How is the Holy Spirit leading me to pray?

Week Eight

THIRTY SECONDS TO FAME

So teach us to number our days, that we may gain a heart of wisdom.

—Psalm 90:12

I once did a sermon series called "Reality TV Gets Religion," in which I used the FOX network television show *30 Seconds to Fame* as one of the message titles. On the show, contestants had thirty seconds to impress the judges with their talent. Seeing the participants trying to make the best of it within the restricted time reminded me of the life we are challenged to live.

The average American's life expectancy is around 75 years. While that's more than the biblical allotment of "three-score years and ten" (Psalm 90:10, KJV), in the grand scheme of things, it's still short. Heeding the instructions to number our days, I did some counting of my own. If I'm average, I only have twelve thousand days left—and that's not a lot of time.

So, if it is true that we were created with a purpose and that we should live our best life—and I believe it is—then learning to appreciate our limited time becomes essential to fulfilling God's plan for our lives.

Numbering our days not only allows us to assign value to our time, it also allows us to "gain a heart of wisdom" (Psalm 90:12, NKJV), as the Bible suggests. And if we are wise, we will know that we were created for good works, which God prepared beforehand that we should walk in them, and that anything done here, any time spent here, is only preparatory to our eternity with God.

—**Jarvis**

Reflect …
What is God saying to me?

Respond …
In response to the devotional, how can I reflect Jesus in my actions?

This week I will …

-

-

-

How is the Holy Spirit leading me to pray?

Week Nine

It's How You Finish

To God our Savior, who alone is wise, be glory and majesty, dominion and power, both now and forever. Amen.
—Jude 1:25

I love my family! But I've learned that just because they're family doesn't mean they support everything I do—even if it's the right thing. Such was the case with Jude.

Jude wrote one of the most inspiring praise hymns in the Bible. It is absolutely beautiful. I get excited just reading it: "Now unto Him who is able to keep you from stumbling, and to present you faultless before the presence of His glory, with exceeding joy, to God our Savior who alone is wise, be glory and majesty, dominion and power, both now and forever." Wow! Now that's praise, and a great way to end a letter. But Jude didn't always have such amazing sentiments.

Jude identifies himself as the brother of James, which makes him also the brother of Jesus. And like James, Jude did not initially believe in the message of Jesus. It wasn't until after the resurrection that Jude came to believe that his brother, Jesus, was who He said He was. Something must have happened to bring about Jude's change of heart. Something transformed this unsupportive family member into a believing brother, willing to fight for the faith.

Whatever happened to Jude, I pray that it also happens to others so that their beginnings, whether great or small, might be transformed into triumphant praise. Because it's not how you start that matters—it's how you finish.

—Jarvis

Reflect ...
What is God saying to me?

Respond ...
In response to the devotional, how can I reflect Jesus in my actions?

This week I will ...

-
-
-

How is the Holy Spirit leading me to pray?

Week Ten

COFFEE-BEAN WOMEN

Then came the daughters of Zelophehad ... And they stood before ... the leaders and all the congregation ... saying: "... Why should the name of our father be removed from among his family because he had no son? Give us a possession among our father's brothers."
—Numbers 27:1–4

If you know the story, you will know that prior to this request, the laws for inheritance allowed only for the division of land among sons. Daughters were not included in the settlement of estates. This carried huge implications because the Israelites were preparing to enter the land that God had promised to give them.

Never before had this been done. There was no history, no tradition, and no example to support this request. Yet these women were courageous enough to ask those in charge why their family would not be able to enjoy the promises of God just because their father had no sons.

In the end, God revealed to Moses that the daughters were right. And in the end, they changed the course of history—they made it better. These women reacted to a critically important situation the way coffee beans react in hot water. They change the water. In fact, their true gifts for change are not released until the water gets hot. How about you?

When Jesus asks us to be salt and light, He's asking us to be agents of change, to be like the daughters of Zelophehad—coffee-bean women. Will you accept the call?

—**Jarvis**

Reflect …
What is God saying to me?

Respond …
In response to the devotional, how can I reflect Jesus in my actions?

This week I will …

-

-

-

How is the Holy Spirit leading me to pray?

Week Eleven

What's in a Name?

And Abraham called the name of the place, The-LORD-Will-Provide; as it is said to this day, "In the Mount of the LORD it shall be provided."

—Genesis 22:14

Have you ever thought about the importance of your name? A friend with a prominent last name once suggested that no one ever thinks about their name until someone in the family does something extraordinarily good or terribly bad. The Bible's wisest man, Solomon, thought that having a good name was "rather to be chosen than great riches." (Proverbs 22:1, KJV)

Apparently for biblical characters, choosing a name extended to more than just people. When Abraham was preparing to offer his son Isaac as a sacrifice to God, a ram suddenly appeared nearby. So Abraham chose to call that place by the name he knew best for God: "My Provider." What's in a name? Or better yet, what's in your name for God?

It's been said that one's relationship with God is tight when that person has a personal descriptive name for God. What do you call God? "My Healer" ... or is it "My Deliverer"? Maybe God is your "Strong Tower," or your "Rock in a Weary Land." Like Abraham, I call God "Jehovah-Jireh" because I know that the Lord will provide!

Perhaps you don't have a name for God yet. May I offer that there is a name above all names; a name that will one day cause every tongue to confess that the bearer of said name is Lord and Savior. If you need a name for God, the name "Jesus" is a good place to start.

—**Jarvis**

Reflect …
What is God saying to me?

Respond …
In response to the devotional, how can I reflect Jesus in my actions?

This week I will …

-

-

-

How is the Holy Spirit leading me to pray?

Week Twelve

GOD WILLING

Come now, you who say, "Today or tomorrow we will go to such and such town ..." yet you do not know what tomorrow will bring ... Instead you ought to say, "If the Lord wills ..."
—James 4:13–15

Church history records that the Puritans had a practice of ending their correspondence with "D.V.," signifying the Latin phrase Deo Volente: "as God wills." The early Methodists also were fond of this custom. And so were lots of people in rural Virginia where I grew up. Actually, they were fond of saying it, not writing it (and not in Latin)—but they sure did say it plenty. "God willing" was used at the end of practically every affirmative answer about future events. "Will you be at church tomorrow?" "Yes sir, God willing."

Currently there is much talk about the future—and rightly so. There are many serious issues without resolution that make our future uncertain. The most vigorous discussion, though, at least for the moment, is about the kind of leadership needed to meet the challenges that the future will present. And most everyone has an opinion.

James was of the opinion that life is short. So rather than saying, "Today or tomorrow we will go to such and such city," he encouraged his first-century audience to instead say, "If the Lord wills, we shall live and do this or that."

The takeaway for us might be best captured in this chorus: "Many things about tomorrow I don't understand; but I know Who holds tomorrow, and I know Who holds my hand." D.V.

—**Jarvis**

Reflect ...
What is God saying to me?

Respond ...
In response to the devotional, how can I reflect Jesus in my actions?

This week I will ...

-

-

-

How is the Holy Spirit leading me to pray?

Week Thirteen

Finish the Race

I have fought the good fight, I have finished the race, I have kept the faith. Finally, there is laid up for me the crown of righteousness ... and not to me only but also to all who have loved His appearing.
—2 Timothy 4:7–8

I watched her struggle to keep up with the other runners. Falling behind, her face became contorted, possibly from pain or as a result of her disability. The other runners struggled, too. But there was something captivating about this girl. As her pace slowed to an awkward walk, the excited crowd cheered louder.

At the halfway mark, the youngster slowed almost to a stop. And as she began to wobble, she drifted sideways toward the edge of the track. Immediately, the girl's father leaped from his seat and rushed to guide his daughter's path. The crowd rose to its feet with applause. As I continued to watch, I realized that everyone in the stadium was focused on that little girl finishing the race. Nothing else seemed to matter.

It didn't matter that on her first step she fell to the ground. It didn't matter that her effort to run was so strained that it was difficult to watch. It didn't matter that she needed assistance to stay on course and in the race. All that mattered was that she finish. And when she did, the crowd erupted. It was perhaps the most glorious celebration I have ever witnessed. All because one little girl finished her race.

That day, all the runners finished their race. And in the celebration, we all knew what the Apostle Paul was saying. Finish the race!

—**Jarvis**

Reflect …
What is God saying to me?

Respond …
In response to the devotional, how can I reflect Jesus in my actions?

This week I will …

-
-
-

How is the Holy Spirit leading me to pray?

Week Fourteen

More Than Enough

But He said to me, "My grace is sufficient for you."
—2 Corinthians 12:9

Not long ago a friend told me, as I vented about a challenge I was having, that I needed an intervention. He was trying to be humorous. But from my perspective, an intervention would have been welcome.

In the history of God's people, we read often about some amazing interventions. Remember when Hezekiah was deathly ill, and prayed facing the wall—and God added fifteen years to his life? Or how about the time Elijah was doing battle with the prophets of Baal—and God sent a firestorm as a demonstration of power?

And then there's this one ... Paul, a "bondservant of Jesus Christ," (Romans 1:1, NKJV) in a moment of physical need, begs the Lord three times for relief. And the response? No intervention. Just this: "My grace is sufficient for you." In other words, God's unmerited favor is enough.

Now, as I look back over two decades of ministry and marriage, I realize that God's grace is not just sufficient—it's more than enough. Because of grace, I am blessed disproportionately to what I deserve. Because of grace, in spite of everything, God chose me.

If you need your situation changed and you're looking for a miracle, know that God already intervened in the person of Jesus—and His grace, and peace, and joy, and everything else He offers, is way more than enough.

—**Jarvis**

Reflect ...
What is God saying to me?

Respond ...
In response to the devotional, how can I reflect Jesus in my actions?

This week I will ...

-
-
-

How is the Holy Spirit leading me to pray?

Week Fifteen

A Work in Progress

Being confident of this very thing, that He who has begun a good work in you will complete it until the day of Jesus Christ.
—Philippians 1:6

"If I've told you once, I've told you a thousand times ..."

That statement doesn't exactly make sense to me, but I know exactly what it means. And I know exactly how my wife feels when she says it. Frustrated! Frustrated because she knows the people she's saying it to aren't doing what she knows they know they should. As a pastor, I sometimes feel that way, too.

It can be very frustrating to serve in a teaching, caring role and not always see tangible, measurable results. The habitual repetition of the same blunder—or worse, the regression from successes previously achieved—is often vexing. Admittedly, some of my unnecessary annoyance is a result of my personality. I often transfer my sometimes unrealistic expectations onto other people. But the real explanation, the one nobody likes to hear, is that we all have issues. That's right. I've got mine, and you've got yours. The good news is that God knows we all are works in progress, and He loves us anyway.

The prophet Jeremiah pointed out that God's people were like clay in a potter's hands. An imperfect vessel can be remade—if not once, then a thousand times. Because I am confident that "He who has begun a good work" in me will finish it when Christ returns, I have "the serenity to accept the things I cannot change," and the "courage to change the things I can." I am a work in progress—and so are you.

—**Jarvis**

Reflect ...
What is God saying to me?

Respond ...
In response to the devotional, how can I reflect Jesus in my actions?

This week I will ...

-

-

-

How is the Holy Spirit leading me to pray?

Week Sixteen

Unity Is Power

"Behold, they are one people, ... and this is only the beginning of what they will do. And nothing that they propose to do will now be impossible for them."
—Genesis 11:6

"Better Together" was the church theme chosen for 2008. It's a great theme, one about which you won't get much argument. There seems to be general agreement that people are designed to be better together—to live in community, or as the Bible proclaims, "to dwell together in unity." (Psalm 133:1, KJV)

While we may be more familiar with the Bible's story through individual characters, God's Word is filled with examples of people working in unity. Jesus said: "Where two or three are gathered together in My name, I am there in the midst of them." (Matthew 18:20, NKJV) And I'm sure you recall what happened in the book of Acts on the day of Pentecost, when the people were in one accord: they were all filled with the Holy Spirit and began to speak in tongues.

It is often said that where there is unity, there is power. I believe that's true. It is also said that power can corrupt. That's true, too—as was the case with the people at Babel. The Bible declares that they had become one, and thus nothing was impossible for them. But they were unified around their own sinful desire to hinder the will of God. So God intervened.

Henry Ford said, "Coming together is a beginning. Keeping together is progress. Working together is success."[3] As you activate the power of unity in your life, seek to know and do the will of God, so that your efforts will be both blessed and a blessing to others.

—Jarvis

Reflect ...
What is God saying to me?

Respond ...
In response to the devotional, how can I reflect Jesus in my actions?

This week I will ...

-

-

-

How is the Holy Spirit leading me to pray?

Week Seventeen

Pray for Peace

And seek the peace of the city where I have caused you to be carried away captive, and pray to the LORD for it; for in its peace you will have peace.
—Jeremiah 29:7

The year was 1940, and the world was in turmoil, preparing to go to war with itself—again.

The Soviet Union, under the leadership of Joseph Stalin, had signed an order calling for the execution of more than twenty-five thousand Polish citizens.

Hitler and Mussolini had initiated the Axis Power in alliance against France and the United Kingdom.

The Third Reich was on the rise, and the Holocaust had begun.

As a result of the German blitzkrieg, British Prime Minister Chamberlain had resigned, and Winston Churchill was now leading the United Kingdom.

In the United States, the nation was divided over the war. African-Americans, in the shadow of Jim Crow, were still fighting to become first-class citizens.

In one of his well-known "Fireside Chats," President Franklin D. Roosevelt, serving his fourth term (the only person to hold that distinction), closed with this: "Day and night, I pray for the restoration of peace in this mad world of ours. It is not necessary that I, the president, ask the American people to pray in behalf of such a cause—for I know you are praying with me."4 If the prophet Jeremiah can ask a people to pray for the peace of a city in which they are held captive, and FDR can call a nation to pray for peace when all around, there is no peace, then I am confident that you will join me now, during our difficult days, to also pray for peace.

—Jarvis

Reflect ...
What is God saying to me?

Respond ...
In response to the devotional, how can I reflect Jesus in my actions?

This week I will ...

-

-

-

How is the Holy Spirit leading me to pray?

Week Eighteen

A Different Way

Then, being divinely warned in a dream that they should not return to Herod, they departed for their own country another way.

—Matthew 2:12

All Christians—and lots of other people, too—know the Christmas story. Whenever someone mentions it to me, I think of my childhood days as a shepherd in the church play, complete with bathrobe and a towel as headgear. And whoever played Mary always brought a doll from home to be baby Jesus.

However you remember it, the Christmas story is an essential part of the Christian faith. This was, and is, an important event: "For there is born to you this day in the city of David a Savior, who is Christ the Lord." Something else important happened in the story, an occurrence that gives additional insight to the significance and meaning of Christ's birth, and one that has happened regularly ever since.

According to the story, wise men who had come to Jerusalem looking for Jesus were commissioned by a troubled King Herod to verify the facts. After finding and worshipping the newborn King, they were divinely warned not to return to Herod. So they departed for their country another way.

As a result of divine intervention, they made a change in their direction. They went to see Jesus one way, and returned another. When humanity meets divinity, something happens. A person cannot have a true encounter with God and stay the same. You may go in one way, but most assuredly, you will come out a different way.

—**Jarvis**

Reflect ...
What is God saying to me?

Respond ...
In response to the devotional, how can I reflect Jesus in my actions?

This week I will ...

-

-

-

How is the Holy Spirit leading me to pray?

Week Nineteen

My Inheritance

I have been reminded of your sincere faith, which first lived in your grandmother Lois and in your mother Eunice and, I am persuaded, now lives in you also.
—2 Timothy 1:5

I had the honor of eulogizing both of my grandmothers. I prayed much before, during, and after each occasion, and they were bittersweet moments for me. Although I struggled each time with making the decision to do the eulogy, looking back, I'm glad I did it. Those experiences with my grandmas are now a part of my inheritance.

I have a few things around the house that I received from my grandmothers. They have little, if any, monetary value. But to me, they are priceless. Even more valuable than the few odds and ends they left me are the values they instilled in me and the examples they set for me. They were both extraordinary women who served their neighbors, their families, and their God. These values, also, are a part of my inheritance.

When Paul writes to Timothy, he gives thanks for Timothy's faith. But he also references the faith of Timothy's mother and his grandmother. The way I read it, Paul is persuaded that Timothy has real faith because Timothy's mother and grandmother had it first. It was a part of his inheritance.

An inheritance is the acquisition of a possession, condition, or trait that is passed from one generation to the next. Thank you, grandmothers, for the stuff, but thanks most for the stuff beyond measure. That's truly my inheritance.

—Jarvis

Reflect ...
What is God saying to me?

Respond ...
In response to the devotional, how can I reflect Jesus in my actions?

This week I will ...

-

-

-

How is the Holy Spirit leading me to pray?

Week Twenty

Chickens Can't Fly

But those who wait on the Lord will find new strength. They will fly high on wings like eagles. They will run and not grow weary. They will walk and not faint.
—Isaiah 40:31

A friend once sent me a card with the caption, "Chickens Can't Fly," on the front. My first thought was that actually, chickens can fly—just not very well or very far. But that wasn't the point. The card was about how to choose friends. There was a reference to the adage, "birds of a feather flock together," and a reminder to always surround oneself with people of character.

Often we humans use animals as examples. And while not everything correlates into a lesson we can use, sometimes animal behavior does provide meaningful learning opportunities. Since the film March of the Penguins was released, I've read or heard several stories edifying the parenting skills and family dynamic of penguins. And perhaps you're familiar with the story, "Lessons Learned from Geese"—lots of motivational speakers use that one.

Another animal frequently used in object lessons is the eagle. Its regal presence, freedom, strength, and reputation as the king of birds make it a fitting symbol for greatness. Isaiah references the eagle's wings. They are quite large, which enables the eagle to use wind currents and even turbulence to soar.

The note attached to my friend's card suggested that "God calls and has made us to be eagles, and even in stormy weather, if we wait on the Lord, we can still fly high." I think he was saying that because I was an eagle, I shouldn't peck with the chickens—because chickens can't fly.

—**Jarvis**

Reflect ...
What is God saying to me?

Respond ...
In response to the devotional, how can I reflect Jesus in my actions?

This week I will ...

-

-

-

How is the Holy Spirit leading me to pray?

Week Twenty-One

The Old Landmark

Then the king ... made a covenant before the LORD, to follow the LORD and to keep His commandments and His testimonies and His statutes ... to perform the words of this covenant that were written in this book. And all the people took a stand for the covenant.
—2 Kings 23:3

There's a song that says: "Let us all go back to the old landmark, then we'll stay in the service of the Lord." As a person who tends to be progressive, talk of "going back" gets my attention. However, going back to reclaim something to help us move forward might be a good idea.

So it was with King Josiah. During his reign, the people had strayed away and forgotten about God's ways. One day, while repair work was going on at the temple, the workers made a landmark discovery: the lost Book of the Law was found. The king was so moved that he had the book read before all the people. Then he called for a return to God's commandments, testimonies, and statutes.

A landmark literally means a geographic feature used to find one's way back or through an area, or a recognizable feature used as a reference point for navigation. King Josiah used God's word as a landmark to remind the people of the godly principles that had once been their guide, and to give them renewed enthusiasm for following the ways of God.

If you need some direction and you're looking for a landmark, Jesus said this: "I am the way." Jesus is my "old landmark"; I invite you to make Him yours.

—Jarvis

Reflect ...
What is God saying to me?

Respond ...
In response to the devotional, how can I reflect Jesus in my actions?

This week I will ...

-
-
-

How is the Holy Spirit leading me to pray?

Week Twenty-Two

MERITORIOUS SERVICE

Though He slay me, yet will I trust Him ...
—Job 13:15

While in the army, I received an award for meritorious service. I now proudly display the certificate on the wall in my office. But what I did—my act of service—I didn't do for any kind of reward. And with or without the recognition, I would do it again.

In the drama between God and Satan captured in the book of Job, Satan accuses Job of serving God for material gain. As the story unfolds, Job's faith is tested even to the point of questioning God. Have you ever been where Job was—doing the right thing but having difficulties, and wondering why it's happening to you? In the end, after losing all that he cherished, Job was still able to declare: "Though He slay me, yet will I trust Him."

The framed certificate hanging on my wall is simply beautiful. Every time I read the citation, I feel good inside. But the service I rendered for my country, in a hostile environment, was done because I believed in something greater than myself. Job likewise served meritoriously, withstanding the fierce attack of the enemy, because he too believed in something and Someone greater than himself.

If you're feeling under attack, know that God is bigger than any situation you may be facing. To serve meritoriously, just remember these words from the hymn writer Civilla Martin: "Be not dismayed whate're betide, God will take care of you ..."[5]

—Jarvis

Reflect ...
What is God saying to me?

Respond ...
In response to the devotional, how can I reflect Jesus in my actions?

This week I will ...

-

-

-

How is the Holy Spirit leading me to pray?

Week Twenty-Three

A Sure Foundation

"Whoever comes to Me, and hears My sayings and does them, I will show you whom he is like: He is like a man building a house, who dug deep and laid the foundation on the rock. And when the flood arose, the stream beat vehemently against that house, and could not shake it, for it was founded on the rock."
—Luke 6:47–48

What kind of house do you live in? There are many different types. I live in a ranch-style home. And I remember when it was being built. I was on site at least once a day, usually several times daily. The builder once asked if I wanted to come and work for him. I must have seen every nail hammered, every block laid, and every square inch of dirt moved. My house plans called for a basement, so there was much dirt being moved.

As I watched the large amounts of earth being dug out and carried away from where my house was supposed to be, I grew concerned that my home would not sit properly on the terrain—that it would be too low. When I shared my uneasiness with the builder, here's what he said: "Your property is on a spot once used to dump fill dirt, and I could certainly build your house on top of that—lots of builders do. But I prefer to dig down to the original dirt. That way I know the foundation is on solid ground."

Jesus suggested in the parable that anyone who followed His teaching was like the man whose house was "founded on the rock"—it would not be washed away by the storm. In these unsure times, the only sure foundation is Jesus, the Rock of Ages. Don't get demolished by the storm—build on the Rock.

—**Jarvis**

Reflect …
What is God saying to me?

Respond …
In response to the devotional, how can I reflect Jesus in my actions?

This week I will …

-

-

-

How is the Holy Spirit leading me to pray?

Week Twenty-Four

THOSE CRAZY CHRISTIANS

But we preach Christ crucified, a stumbling block to Jews and foolishness to the Gentiles.
—1 Corinthians 1:23

Someone who knew my seminary history and knew my sense of humor sent me this story about the Dean of the Chapel:

Will Willimon was approached one Sunday after chapel by a student who wanted to know if she had to believe in the virgin birth in order to be a Christian.

"No," said Willimon, "you don't.

"But," he went on, "if we can get you to swallow that without choking, then there's no telling what we can get you to believe. Come back next week and we'll try to persuade you that the meek will inherit the earth; that it is better to give than to receive; that your life does not consist in the abundance of possessions; that it's not nations, or empires, not even the United States, but God who rules the world."

Said Willimon: "We start you out with something fairly small, like the virgin birth, and then work you up to even more outrageous assertions."

My friend was right about my humor—I absolutely loved this story. Dean Willimon was also right. We Christians have some truly outrageous assertions. That reminds me of a headline that appeared in the local newspaper. It read: "Jesus Loves Strippers, Too"—another outrageous assertion.

But here's the really shocking claim. To demonstrate His love, God sent His Son to die on a cross so that you, me, strippers, and everyone else could have an opportunity to live forever. Now that's outrageous! As Paul wrote, to those who are perishing, the message of the cross is foolishness; but to those of us who are being saved, it is the power of God. So if that's crazy—count me in.

—**Jarvis**

Reflect …
What is God saying to me?

Respond …
In response to the devotional, how can I reflect Jesus in my actions?

This week I will …

-
-
-

How is the Holy Spirit leading me to pray?

# Week Twenty-Five

AUTHENTIC MANHOOD

Be strong, therefore, and prove yourself a man. And keep the charge of the LORD your God: to walk in His ways ... that you may prosper in all that you do and wherever you turn.
—1 Kings 2:2–3

My dad made sure I understood that "just being male doesn't make you a man." We talked a lot about that subject, especially once I became interested in girls. He used words like "responsibility," "respect," and "self-control."

It's important for fathers to tell their sons about authentic manhood. My sons have heard the speech so much they should know it by heart. Solomon, before he became king, received a final father-son talk from his dying dad about manhood. David suggested to his son, Solomon, that he should prove his manhood.

David knew from experience that becoming an authentic man was not easy—that it required tempering courage with compassion, and strength with service. He also knew that Solomon would fail in his attempt at authentic manhood if he did not maintain obedient fellowship with God. So he told him: "Keep the charge of the LORD your God, to walk in His ways ... that you may prosper in all that you do."

The need for authentic manhood in our society is great. "Authentic" means genuine, true, or real. Authentic men—real men—are men of character. They bring honor to the word father... and respect to the word brother. They are men whose parents say, "We're glad he is our son," and whose wife says, "I'm glad he's my husband." If David were alive today, I think he would add: "Real men love Jesus."

—**Jarvis**

Reflect ...
What is God saying to me?

Respond ...
In response to the devotional, how can I reflect Jesus in my actions?

This week I will ...

-

-

-

How is the Holy Spirit leading me to pray?

Week Twenty-Six

It Ain't Always About Us

The LORD had said ... I will make you into a great nation and I will bless you; I will make your name great, and you will be a blessing.
—Genesis 12:1–2

I once heard that people have to read something seven times before they get it. Actually, it may take more than that for me. I have read the story of Abram many times, and gleaned from it many lessons. But I was beyond the seventh reading before it dawned on me that when God was blessing Abram, God's immediate priority may have been someone other than Abram.

Admittedly, I sometimes get caught up in that culture where everything appears to be about me. I view the world through the same "I-glasses" that are popular with many people. But as I read Abram's story again, I realize that I (like Abram) am not the only person on God's mind. "It ain't always about us."

Abram was a blessed man. He walked before God, and he witnessed the movement of God many times. God personally told Abram: "I will bless you and make your name great." Then God added: "And you shall be a blessing." Abram was "B2B"—blessed to be a blessing. God's plan to bless "all the families of the earth" flowed through Abram.

The next time you feel compelled to shout: "I'm blessed!" consider that God's intention for blessing you may have more to do with someone else. Remember, "It ain't always about you." You are blessed to be a blessing.

—**Jarvis**

Reflect …
What is God saying to me?

Respond …
In response to the devotional, how can I reflect Jesus in my actions?

This week I will …

-

-

-

How is the Holy Spirit leading me to pray?

Week Twenty-Seven

Teach Us to Pray

One of his disciples said to him, "Lord, teach us to pray, as John taught his disciples."
—Luke 11:1

There's a story in the Bible about prayer that goes something like this: Jesus was off in a certain place engaged in personal prayer time. When he had finished praying, one of his disciples asked Him, "Lord, teach us to pray." So Jesus replied: "When you pray say this ..." He continued with what we now refer to as the "Lord's Prayer."

This model prayer has become a staple in the Christian faith. It is embedded in our memories, and used over and again by many. And that's good. Yet, I believe the disciples' request was more comprehensive than a desire to know the right words to one prayer. Their request, I believe, was for Jesus to model for them a prayerful lifestyle, and to expose them to the true meaning and nature of prayer. Teach us how to pray, and also teach us to pray.

So their request also becomes ours: "Lord, teach us to pray." Instill in us the knowledge that there is something greater than ourselves, and therein lies the source of our strength. Endow us with a spirit that allows us to look beyond our circumstances to that hope that defies logic and exists outside what we can explain in the natural. Most of all, Lord, give us a desire and a willingness to humble ourselves, to turn away from sin, and to seek Your face.

Lord, teach us to pray.

—**Jarvis**

Reflect ...
What is God saying to me?

Respond ...
In response to the devotional, how can I reflect Jesus in my actions?

This week I will ...

-
-
-

How is the Holy Spirit leading me to pray?

Week Twenty-Eight

THE REAL WORLD

Then Jesus said, "Come to me, all of you who are weary and carry heavy burdens, and I will give you rest."
—Matthew 11:28

"Welcome to the desert of the real." I love that line from the movie The Matrix. It seems applicable to the ministry of Jesus, who was most likely to be found serving the real needs of real people when their lives may have seemed very much like a desert.

I do realize that life's not always bad. In fact, my life (and maybe yours, too) has been pretty good. But there are times when we, as my wife would say, "just want to lie down and cry." And for the most part, we don't admit when life is hard—and sometimes it is very hard.

Once I had to make a two-hour car repair in the middle of a rainstorm. It was at night, it was cold, and I had a commitment I had to keep. Simply put, I wanted to lie down and cry. And you know what? It's OK to feel that way. Lots of people do, but they won't acknowledge it. The good news is that you don't have to be perfect to have a relationship with God. In fact, Jesus said, "The Son of Man has come to save that which was lost."

In the real world, there is joy and pain. Life can be good, but sometimes we get hurt and we lose our way. We can manage by ourselves in the good times, but during the rainstorm—that's when we need a refuge. And that's what is really cool about Jesus, who says we can bring all our cares and concerns to Him, and He will give us rest. That's the real deal.

—**Jarvis**

Reflect ...
What is God saying to me?

Respond ...
In response to the devotional, how can I reflect Jesus in my actions?

This week I will ...

-

-

-

How is the Holy Spirit leading me to pray?

Week Twenty-Nine

Ready for Community?

Let nothing be done through selfish ambition or conceit, but in lowliness of mind let each esteem others better than himself.
—Philippians 2:3

The first section in John Maxwell's book, Winning with People, is titled, "The Readiness Question: Are We Prepared for Relationships?" I asked a similar question of those preparing to plant a new church that would have "Community" in its name and would hold relationships as its highest priority. Establishing community was the right thing to do, and it sounded great. But after hearing Gordon Venturella say in a sermon on community that "it demands your sacrifice and requires the forfeiture of your rights and preferences," I wasn't sure any of us were ready for true community.

That's the thing with us and our faith. It all sounds great. But are we really ever ready? I mean, love and forgiveness are beautiful things. But it's hard to put those into practice. Trust me, I know. And building real community takes patience and time. Now, do we really want to give up our time? And community is based on relationships, and relationships require sacrifice. Well, that's just about more than most are willing to give.

Jesus understood this, so to help us know Him better, He told us that He came not to be served, but to serve others. Jesus spent His ministerial career esteeming others more than Himself. And to reveal to us the nature of true community and to give us a chance to have the definitive relationship, Jesus made the supreme sacrifice: He gave His life in exchange for ours. Are you really ready for community?

—**Jarvis**

Reflect ...
What is God saying to me?

Respond ...
In response to the devotional, how can I reflect Jesus in my actions?

This week I will ...

-

-

-

How is the Holy Spirit leading me to pray?

Week Thirty

BEGINNING AT THE END

Therefore, if anyone is in Christ, he is a new creation; old things have passed away; behold, all things have become new.
—2 Corinthians 5:17

After many days of constant bombing, the word finally came for the forces on the ground to begin the assault. We said our last prayers, mounted the vehicles, and rolled out into the desert sun and sand. All day, all night, and into the next day, our convoy moved forward, stopping only to refuel and to change drivers. And then, as suddenly as we had started, we came to a screeching halt.

"What's going on?" my assistant asked.

We could hear yelling and see what appeared to be dancing by the occupants of the vehicles up at the front. Finally, we received the word: "Hussein surrendered! The war is over!"

Afterwards, one of the soldiers made this simple, somewhat familiar statement: "Today is the best, first day of the rest of my life." This sentiment of a new beginning from this day forward was shared by many, I'm sure. And it was all made possible because of an ending. It was a beginning at the end.

I once heard someone say, "We are people of beginnings. We celebrate beginnings, but we want to forget endings." As a follower of Jesus, though, there's more to the story. We love new beginnings, but we love endings, too. Because we know that dawn follows the midnight, daylight follows the darkness, and life follows death. And we celebrate with the passing of old things, "behold, all things have become new."

—Jarvis

Reflect ...
What is God saying to me?

Respond ...
In response to the devotional, how can I reflect Jesus in my actions?

This week I will ...

-
-
-

How is the Holy Spirit leading me to pray?

Week Thirty-One

BY OUR LOVE

"By this all people will know that you are My disciples, if you have love for one another."
—John 13:35

During a church sanctuary dedication, the keynote speaker asked the congregants, "What kind of religion will you practice in this place—hurting or healing? Practice what you preach."

Christians, like any other group, are known for their habits and practices—good and bad. Before Jesus departed this earth, He reminded His followers how they should be known.

Around the fellowship tables that evening, people humorously discussed the traits by which familiar organizations are recognized. I dare not reveal my affiliations. But I will admit that in some cases I joined them for their reputation. Jesus said that his followers would also have a reputation.

So, how will others know that you are His disciples? Will they know because they see you going to church regularly? Will they know because they go to church with you, and hear your beautiful songs and prayers or observe that you accurately quote Scripture? Will they know because they observe that you are a spiritual person? No, I don't think so. Jesus declared: "By this all will know that you are My disciples, if you have love for one another."

The first time I heard it, I loved it. Anna sang it softly, playing the chords on her guitar as the rest of the group harmonized, and it was sweet: "And they'll know we are Christians by our love, by our love. Yes, they'll know we are Christians by our love."

—Jarvis

Reflect ...
What is God saying to me?

Respond ...
In response to the devotional, how can I reflect Jesus in my actions?

This week I will ...

-

-

-

How is the Holy Spirit leading me to pray?

Week Thirty-Two

It's Your Availability

And the Syrians had gone out on raids, and had brought back captive a young girl from the land of Israel ... And Naaman went in and told his master, saying, "Thus and thus said the girl who is from the land of Israel."
—2 Kings 5:2–4

In the end, Naaman gets miraculously healed from his disease. But Naaman, captain of the Syrian army, is not the hero of the story. Elisha, the man of God responsible for administering the healing, is not the hero, either. He was doing his job. The real heroes are "nobodies" whose names don't even appear in the story. We only know them by their position: servants. But it's not about their ability. It's their availability that matters.

First there was the young girl taken captive from Israel who had been given to Naaman's wife as a maid. My guess is that she did not want to be there at all—she was taken from her home and forced into servitude. But there she was, available to be used by God. Because of her, Naaman found out that there was a man who could heal his disease.

Then there were Naaman's servants. All we know about them is that they were with Naaman. But because they were there, when he did not believe the prophet, they were able to encourage Naaman to follow the instructions of God's man and be healed. It wasn't the servants' ability, but their availability that made the difference.

Whoever, wherever, or whatever you think you are or are not, know this: God can use you! Because of the nameless characters in the story, a man's life was changed forever. But their names now appear in another story. And yours can, too. Because it's not always your ability that matters—it's your availability.

—**Jarvis**

Reflect ...
What is God saying to me?

Respond ...
In response to the devotional, how can I reflect Jesus in my actions?

This week I will ...

-

-

-

How is the Holy Spirit leading me to pray?

Week Thirty-Three

Do It!

And Jabez called on the God of Israel saying, "Oh, that You would bless me indeed, and enlarge my territory ..." So God granted him what he requested.
—1 Chronicles 4:10

The Prayer of Jabez created quite a stir. It was a great book. I run into people all the time who now have the prayer posted on something personal or visible. The highlight of the prayer for me was that God gave Jabez everything he asked for.

From the prayer, the most frequent request I hear is the one for God to "expand my territory." Many people seem to want to live large for God. They get excited when they talk about the possibilities. But when I see them months, even years, later, they're still praying for the expansion. Again, what strikes me is that God gave Jabez everything he asked for—including the expanded territory.

Maybe God has already given us our territory, too. But we don't know how to possess it. For many years I didn't know how to possess my expanded territory, either. I knew I was supposed to do something extraordinary for God. I had even seen the vision. But occupying the land was a different matter altogether. Then I remembered some two-word commands God used on the Israelites to move them into their promised land.

God told Abram to "get out." He told Moses to "go in." And God told Joshua to "get up" and "go over." All of this just to get them to a place He had already promised. Has God already answered your prayer? Go possess your territory. Do it!

—**Jarvis**

Reflect ...
What is God saying to me?

Respond ...
In response to the devotional, how can I reflect Jesus in my actions?

This week I will ...

-
-
-

How is the Holy Spirit leading me to pray?

Week Thirty-Four

Amazing Faith!

When Jesus saw their faith, He said to the paralytic, "Son, your sins are forgiven."
—Mark 2:5

The Gospels are full of wonderful stories about the life and times of Jesus. He did some really cool things. But this one, about a paralytic man being healed, is one of my favorites.

The story opens with a bang! Word gets out that Jesus is in the house, and the crowd grows larger than the space can hold. While Jesus is preaching, four men approach. They're carrying a paralyzed man. The number of people is too great to allow the men through the doors, so they take the roof off and lower the paralytic man down to Him. Jesus sees the faith of the four men and says to the paralytic, "Son, your sins are forgiven you."

Now, I know that faith is a major component of being a Christ-follower. I know that it is impossible to please God without it. And I, along with every other youngster in Sunday school, learned that "prayer is the key to heaven, but faith unlocks the door." But I thought those were references to personal faith. In this story, Jesus reacts to the faith of others. And there are more stories just like this one.

I don't know what Jesus was trying to prove. But what He did was truly amazing. Some of the eyewitnesses even said: "We never saw anything like this." Looking over my life, I think there were others along the way whose faith made the difference for me: people who carried me to Jesus; people who made sure that I knew Jesus and that Jesus knew me. Now that's amazing faith!

—**Jarvis**

Reflect ...
What is God saying to me?

Respond ...
In response to the devotional, how can I reflect Jesus in my actions?

This week I will ...

-
-
-

How is the Holy Spirit leading me to pray?

Week Thirty-Five

Cash versus Character

But you, man of God, flee from all this, and pursue righteousness, godliness, faith, love, endurance and gentleness.
—*1 Timothy 6:11*

I told him it was important to know when to run.

He replied: "It's also important to know which way to run.

"There are a few things I would want to run towards," he added.

Of course, he was being humorous. But love for money, and Paul's suggestion to run from it, is no laughing matter.

Listen to the preceding verse, 1 Timothy 6:10: "the love of money is a root of all kinds of evil, for which some have strayed from the faith … and pierced themselves through with many sorrows." Now, that's pretty much self-explanatory.

Don't get it twisted, though. Paul isn't saying not to adequately provide for yourself or your family. In fact, I believe that he would agree that a good way not to fall into the greediness trap is by gainful work. What Paul is suggesting is that we keep it in check by pursuing the things of God.

I am constantly shocked and amazed by what people are willing to do for money. But apparently, the issue has been around a long time. When Paul wrote to Timothy, it was a minister-to-minister correspondence. But his advice is good for everyone.

In the battle between cash and character, choose character. Avoid the evils associated with greed, and pursue righteousness. Jesus reminds us that when we seek first the kingdom of God, the material things we need will come. (Matthew 6:33, KJV)

—**Jarvis**

Reflect ...
What is God saying to me?

Respond ...
In response to the devotional, how can I reflect Jesus in my actions?

This week I will ...

-
-
-

How is the Holy Spirit leading me to pray?

Week Thirty-Six

Where's the Fruit?

"Yes, I am the vine; you are the branches. Those who remain in Me, and I in them, will produce much fruit. For apart from Me you can do nothing."
—John 15:5

In the 1980s, the Wendy's fast-food franchise aired a television commercial in which an elderly lady is handed an oversized bun with a tiny burger on it, to which she replies: "Where's the beef?" The slogan quickly became popular as a catch-all phrase used to challenge the size or importance of everything imaginable. Whatever it was, if it didn't measure up, the right response was: "Where's the beef?"

On the night that Jesus was betrayed, at the end of the last supper—just hours before his death—He shared some final, important remarks with His disciples. He anticipated that upon His departure, they would face persecution and be inclined to grow apart, so He told them to love one another. Jesus also instructed them to remain firmly grounded in His ways; they should abide in Him, and He in them. As a result, they would "bear much fruit"—their lives would become the epitome of Christ-like character and behavior.

Modern-day Christ followers are also challenged to bear fruit. Yet considering the fact that many nonbelievers cite hypocrisy and irrelevancy as primary deterrents to conversion, I wonder if we shouldn't be asking ourselves a similar question: "Where's the fruit?" Because Jesus lives, and He lives also in us, we are empowered to be the difference in our world. All should see our fruit and know by its abundance that we are disciples of Christ.

—**Jarvis**

Reflect ...
What is God saying to me?

Respond ...
In response to the devotional, how can I reflect Jesus in my actions?

This week I will ...

-

-

-

How is the Holy Spirit leading me to pray?

Week Thirty-Seven

Hard Work

Even while we were with you, we gave you this rule:
"Whoever does not work should not eat."
—2 Thessalonians 3:10

Growing up, I spent a huge amount of time with my grandfathers. I observed that both of them were very committed to hard work. My paternal grandfather was self-employed. I never knew him to work for anyone other than himself. And even though he worked extremely hard, I knew from watching him that I wanted to someday work for myself.

My mother's father, on the other hand, always had a couple of jobs—and usually a side business for extra cash. At his jobs, he often did more than his fair share of the work. He and my paternal grandfather shared the same commitment to a work ethic and the same belief that hard work was fundamental to good character. These ideals left a great impression on a youngster whose mind was usually on things other than work.

Another benefit: at an early age, I developed an understanding of the relationship between working and eating—as well as the necessity of working to achieve personal success. I recall thinking many times that others may have more talent or resources, but they would have to "go a ways" to out-work me.

Like my granddads, the Bible also has a clear, favorable view regarding work. It speaks against slothfulness and laziness, and advises people to be industrious and productive. And it commands that "if anyone will not work, neither shall they eat." Besides, as Grandpa would say, "a little hard work never hurt anybody."

—**Jarvis**

Reflect ...
What is God saying to me?

Respond ...
In response to the devotional, how can I reflect Jesus in my actions?

This week I will ...

-

-

-

How is the Holy Spirit leading me to pray?

Week Thirty-Eight

The Children Are Our Future

But when Jesus saw it, He was greatly displeased and said to them, "Let the little children come to Me, and do not forbid them; for of such is the kingdom of God."
—Mark 10:14

Jesus loved the little children, and so do I. They give me so much more than I give to them. I love their innocence, their honesty, and their energy. They're great people. Some parents of Jesus's day also recognized how special children were, because they brought them to receive His touch.

The disciples, thinking that it wasn't such a good idea for Jesus to be bothered, rebuked the parents for bringing the children. But this greatly displeased Jesus—in fact, He was angry. We don't often talk about this side of Jesus, but there were times when He let people know that He did not like what was going on. This was one of those times.

Even though ancient culture was not necessarily favorable towards children, Jesus believed that they were the center of life in the kingdom. How we treat children says much about our character and our faith. Are you with Jesus in saying: "let the little children come to Me?"

Here's what I think:

I believe the children are our future,
Teach them well and let them lead the way.
Show them all the beauty they possess inside.
Give them a sense of pride to make it easier.
Let the children's laughter remind us how we used to be.[6]

When people told me, "They grow up fast—cherish every minute with your little ones," I'm glad I listened.

—**Jarvis**

Reflect ...
What is God saying to me?

Respond ...
In response to the devotional, how can I reflect Jesus in my actions?

This week I will ...

-

-

-

How is the Holy Spirit leading me to pray?

Week Thirty-Nine

Good Examples

We give thanks to God always for you all ... remembering without ceasing your work of faith, labor of love, and patience of hope in our Lord Jesus Christ.
—1 Thessalonians 1:2–3

During the farewell celebration for a former U.S. president, I remember being caught up in all the ceremony of the occasion. Watching the traditions unfold—the military processional, the arrivals of dignitaries from all parts of the world, the eulogies from friends and family—reminded me of those special moments when we see the best in people. When we see people connected by an event that creates unity of purpose, we catch a glimpse of what our world could become.

I believe that Paul had similar memories as he thought about and wrote to his friends at the young Thessalonian church. The church's persistence through love, faith, and hope was quite praiseworthy. And for a moment, we catch a glimpse of what a community of believers could become. Paul writes: "You became followers ... of the Lord, having received the word ... with the joy of the Holy Spirit, so that you became examples to all" (verses 6–7).

Some say good examples are hard to find today. I disagree. They are everywhere—they just don't always get the spotlight. More importantly, each individual has the power to become the very best example possible. The Thessalonians understood this. They embraced their new faith and lived it in a way that gave them world renown. They were good examples. For sure, they knew that "If you can't be the sun, be a star / ... / Be the best of whatever you are."[7]

—Jarvis

Reflect ...
What is God saying to me?

Respond ...
In response to the devotional, how can I reflect Jesus in my actions?

This week I will ...

-

-

-

How is the Holy Spirit leading me to pray?

Week Forty

Keep the Faith, Baby

"But I have prayed for you, that your faith should not fail; and when you have returned to Me, strengthen your brethren."
—Luke 22:32

I have had the honor of knowing many great people, not famous or rich, or highly educated or well-traveled, but great nonetheless. One such person gave me, among other things, many pearls of wisdom during our frequent visits while we were neighbors. He lived and dressed very modestly, but his persona was one of nobility. I knew he had worked at a university. Obviously, I thought, as a professor. I later learned that he had been a janitor for forty-five years.

One day when I was feeling frustrated by the many challenges that faced our community, I went to see my friend. We discussed every problem ever experienced in the world. As I walked down the steps to return home, still visibly upset that we had resolved nothing, my very wise friend called to me: "My brother, as Adam Clayton Powell used to say: 'Keep the faith, baby!'"

Immediately, that statement charged through to the very depth of my being. It was as if I could hear the great freedom fighters of old speaking directly to me: "Do not let our struggling be in vain. At any cost, keep the faith, baby." Also, at that moment, I felt secure in knowing that Jesus had anticipated the struggles of discipleship and had prayed for Peter and for us, that our faith should not fail.

And so, if you are having any challenges at all—and even if you're not—I say to you as my great friend and brother said to me: "Keep the faith, baby!"

—**Jarvis**

Reflect ...
What is God saying to me?

Respond ...
In response to the devotional, how can I reflect Jesus in my actions?

This week I will ...

-
-
-

How is the Holy Spirit leading me to pray?

Week Forty-One

A New Thing?

Jesus Christ the same yesterday, and today, and forever.
—Hebrews 13:8

As soon as I read the preface to What the Spirit Is Saying to the Churches, I knew I was going to like it. The topic of the preface is "When God Works." And make no mistake about it—I believe that God is at work! Regardless of the situation, condition, or perspective, I believe God has been, is now, and will continue to be at work in our world.

Lately I've heard a number of people say, "God is doing a new thing." And I have been known to say it, too. But as I've grown spiritually, I have come to understand that God isn't doing a new thing. God is doing the same thing as always—being God. What's new is that I'm experiencing God in a way that's different from before. Something has changed, but it isn't God.

Maybe it's a personal life occurrence … or maybe an historic event … or maybe it's just the right time. Whatever it is, it allows for the development of a new perspective, new insights, or perhaps a new attitude. But, again, it isn't God who changes. And that's good news.

As the church planter of a congregation that celebrates diversity and embraces people's differences, it is reassuring to worship a God who is always the same. My most favorite hymn puts it this way:

Great is Thy faithfulness, O God my Father;
There is no shadow of turning with Thee;
Thou changest not, Thy compassions, they fail not;
As Thou hast been, Thou forever wilt be.8

If you're game, let this unchanging God do a new thing in you.

—Jarvis

Reflect ...
What is God saying to me?

Respond ...
In response to the devotional, how can I reflect Jesus in my actions?

This week I will ...

-

-

-

How is the Holy Spirit leading me to pray?

Week Forty-Two

I Pray For You

Pray for each other ... The earnest prayer of a righteous person has great power and wonderful results.
—James 5:16

I was the planting pastor for a new church that launched in September 2005. The vision of the church, and everything about its formation, was the result of prayer, and the original leadership was determined to establish prayer as the lifeline of the church.

The Bible speaks volumes about the necessity of prayer, and encourages us to pray for one another. But how would we pray for those we hoped to reach in our new community—people with whom we had not yet established relationships—people who we did not yet know?

Sometimes our answers are closer than we think, and some things speak for themselves. When I read Paul's prayer for those he served, I immediately knew it was the perfect prayer for those I would serve in my new place of ministry. I prayed for them, and now I pray for you as Paul prayed for the church in Ephesus (Ephesians 1:17–21 NKJV):

That the God of our Lord Jesus Christ, the Father of glory, may give to you the spirit of wisdom and revelation in the knowledge of Him, the eyes of your understanding being enlightened; that you may know what is the hope of His calling, what are the riches of the glory of His inheritance in the saints, and what is the exceeding greatness of His power toward us who believe, according to the working of His mighty power which He worked in Christ when He raised Him from the dead and seated Him at His right hand in the heavenly places, far above all principality and power and might and dominion, and every name that is named, not only in this age but also in that which is to come.

Amen.

—**Jarvis**

Reflect ...
What is God saying to me?

Respond ...
In response to the devotional, how can I reflect Jesus in my actions?

This week I will ...

-
-
-

How is the Holy Spirit leading me to pray?

Week Forty-Three

Come

And the Spirit and the bride say, "Come!" And let him who hears say, "Come!" And let him who thirsts come. Whoever desires, let him take the water of life freely.
—Revelation 22:17

Have you ever heard "all's well that ends well?" You probably have, and you probably also know that it's the title of a play written by William Shakespeare.

The play is a cross between a love story and a tragedy. In order for an "odd couple" to get together, several unusual circumstances have to occur. To set up the right conditions, there are many twists and turns, ups and downs, and tricks and deceptions in the play. At times, it's even hard to follow the plot. But when it's all said and done, the couple gets together and, as the title suggests, "all's well that ends well."

Our lives, too, may be filled with turns and twists, ups and downs, and tricks and deceptions. If so, we would be no different than those who first heard the words, "let him who thirsts come." They were experiencing enormous persecution because of their faith, and I would imagine that life, at times, was far more confusing for them than for those in the Shakespearean play. But in the end, they are invited to come and "take the water of Life freely."

In Matthew's Gospel, Jesus says: "Come to Me, all you who labor and are heavy laden, and I will give you rest." I've actually been told that "come" may be the greatest word in the Bible. The point is this: wherever you are on your journey, Jesus offers you an invitation to have a well ending—He invites you to come.

And as Granny would say, "Do it now!"

—Jarvis

Reflect ...
What is God saying to me?

Respond ...
In response to the devotional, how can I reflect Jesus in my actions?

This week I will ...

-
-
-

How is the Holy Spirit leading me to pray?

Week Forty-Four

THE SECRET OF SUCCESS

His lord said to him, "Well done, good and faithful servant; you were faithful over a few things, I will make you ruler over many things. Enter into the joy of your lord."
—Matthew 25:21

Lots of people think about success—even desire it. What about you? It is, after all, part of the "American Dream." Isn't it? Aren't we supposed to be successful?

As a young boy, I don't remember anyone ever saying, "Grow up and be a failure!" I do, however, remember being told to be successful. Even now, the adults I know are still engaged by the idea of becoming successful. With so much emphasis on achievement and accomplishment, I've always believed that it's good to have some perspective regarding the meaning of success—not only in our eyes or in the eyes of those around us, but also in the eyes of God.

I like my brother's perspective: "I was doing well climbing the ladder of success. But then I found out that my ladder was leaning against the wrong building." What building is your ladder leaning against—the building of fortune or fame? According to the Bible, God doesn't measure our success by what we have. God measures our success by what we do with what we have.

If you notice in the verse from Matthew, the acknowledgment of a job well done is not based on the size of the accomplishment, but on the commitment to faithfulness. The secret of success, then, is a matter of stewardship. Are you faithful regarding the gifts God has assigned to you? If you are ... well done!

—**Jarvis**

Reflect ...
What is God saying to me?

Respond ...
In response to the devotional, how can I reflect Jesus in my actions?

This week I will ...

-
-
-

How is the Holy Spirit leading me to pray?

Week Forty-Five

A Lesson in Giving

Just then he looked up and saw the rich people dropping offerings in the collection plate. Then he saw a poor widow put in two pennies. He said, "The plain truth is that this widow has given by far the largest offering today. All these others made offerings that they'll never miss; she gave extravagantly what she couldn't afford—she gave her all!"
—Luke 21:1-4

On Sunday, December 1, 1912, Russell Conwell, pastor of Grace Baptist Church in Philadelphia, unveiled for his congregation a picture of little Miss Hattie May Wiatt. Hattie, only a child at the time of her death twenty-six years earlier, had managed to scrape up fifty-seven cents which she had planned to donate toward a new Sunday school building—one that would be large enough to hold all the little children. Hattie's fifty-seven cents became the first gift toward the new building, and a seed of motivation for the pastor and congregation to accomplish many more works in the community.

Even though over the years, the story of the fifty-seven cents has been reshaped and retold many times, it is nonetheless an extraordinary lesson in giving.

Twenty-plus years ago, when I began my journey as a minister, my pastor thought it wise that I should have a lesson in giving. He told me that "giving is a good indicator of spiritual growth and maturity." Like all of my gifts, he said, the ability to give comes from God and should be used to "bless God as well as other people." He finished my lesson with the story of the widow's contribution, and this counsel: my service to God may require self-sacrifice, and sometimes "it's not about what you give, but what you give up."

—**Jarvis**

Reflect ...
What is God saying to me?

Respond ...
In response to the devotional, how can I reflect Jesus in my actions?

This week I will ...

-
-
-

How is the Holy Spirit leading me to pray?

Week Forty-Six

THE RIGHT QUESTION

He asked his disciples, "Who do people say the Son of Man is?" They replied, "Some say ... John the Baptist ... Elijah ... Jeremiah ... one of the prophets." "But what about you?" he asked. "Who do you say I am?"
—Matthew 16:13–15

In the 2004 film I, Robot, the main character, Detective Spooner, attempts to solve the murder of his friend Dr. Lanning, a robotics specialist. The detective is guided by a holographic image of his friend, who continues to suggest that the resolution of the crime is contingent upon asking the right question. As a father, I have experienced firsthand the power of the right question. That question still brings tears to my eyes.

Our two toddlers were quite active, and my wife and I were extremely busy professionally as well as personally. One morning, on my way to drop the children at the daycare, I was venting aloud (actually it was more like whining and complaining) about all the challenges facing me that week.

Then one of my sons asked me from his car seat: "Daddy, doesn't God have the whole world in His hands?"

Well, let me ask you a question: have you ever seen a grown man cry? That morning I wept like a baby, because my son had asked me the right question.

So, here's what I think the right question is, right now. According to Pastor David Guzik, "this is the question placed before all who hear of Jesus; and it is we, not He, who are judged by our answer."9 Simon Peter answered that He is the Christ. But what about you—who do you say that Jesus is? Now that's the right question.

—**Jarvis**

Reflect …
What is God saying to me?

Respond …
In response to the devotional, how can I reflect Jesus in my actions?

This week I will …

-
-
-

How is the Holy Spirit leading me to pray?

Week Forty-Seven

Remember Who You Are

But you are not like that, for you are a chosen people. You are a kingdom of priests, God's holy nation, His very own possession.

—1 Peter 2:9

His voice was calm and low, and he spoke in an even tone: "Remember who you are."

He could tell that I was extremely agitated and upset by the false accusations of the other employees. And it's a good thing that he asked me to step outside the office, because I was at my limit. He continued, "You and I both know you are right, but your conduct has to be different from the other staff members. Remember who you are and what you represent." After taking a few seconds to cool down and think, I agreed.

One of the greatest challenges I have observed among Christians today is the desire to be like everybody else—to fit in; be a part of the culture; talk, dress, act, and even react like the rest of the world, and at the same time adhere to Paul's admonishment not to "conform to this world." But aren't we also asked to be an ambassador—which requires an understanding, even an appreciation, of the culture in order to translate the message of our faith into a culturally relevant format?

For sure, what I almost did and said in that meeting would have been culturally "expectable." But because of who I am in Christ, and because I remembered who I was, I had the opportunity to proclaim the identity and the greatness of God through my actions. I think that's what a good ambassador should do. Do you?

—Jarvis

Reflect ...
What is God saying to me?

Respond ...
In response to the devotional, how can I reflect Jesus in my actions?

This week I will ...

-

-

-

How is the Holy Spirit leading me to pray?

Week Forty-Eight

GIVE THANKS

Rejoice always, pray without ceasing, in everything give thanks: for this is the will of God in Christ Jesus for you.
—1 Thessalonians 5:16–18

Finding clarity in a complex world is not always easy. Among other challenges, questions abound regarding one's purpose and direction in life. If only we knew exactly what God wanted us to do! And while the Bible is our road map to success, we can occasionally miss a turn or misinterpret the directions. So when I encounter a passage that says, "This is the will of God," I'm apt to pay attention.

All right, I thought. Rejoicing, and praying, and giving thanks is great if all is well. But what happens when things are going badly—really badly? The Apostle Paul declares that these actions are not optional—that they are "the will of God." Was I missing something?

According to a friend I greatly admire, I was missing the point entirely. This is what he told me: "The joy I have, the world didn't give it to me. And the world surely can't take it away." He reminded me that our reason for thanksgiving has nothing to do with the results of our living. "It's not about us," he said. "It's about Jesus and what He has done for us."

When Paul wrote to the Thessalonians, he had been forcibly removed from the city under Roman persecution. Yet, he encouraged the people—encourages us—always to give thanks. Regardless of your current situation, remember that in everything we can give thanks, because we have the victory in Christ Jesus.

—Jarvis

Reflect ...
What is God saying to me?

Respond ...
In response to the devotional, how can I reflect Jesus in my actions?

This week I will ...

-
-
-

How is the Holy Spirit leading me to pray?

Week Forty-Nine

Moral Discourse

As iron sharpens iron, so one man sharpens another.
—Proverbs 27:17

This wise saying seems to suggest that there is something to be gained from conscientious dialogue. And I couldn't agree more. As Christian brothers and sisters, we sharpen each other—we hold each other accountable and stir up within each other our God-given gifts and graces. But the benefits of moral discourse extend beyond the individual participants to affect families, neighborhoods, organizations, and even nations.

Franklin D. Roosevelt thought that in order for our civilization to survive, "we must cultivate the science of human relationships—the ability of all people, of all kinds, to live together in the same world at peace." If true, then to achieve this state of meaningful co-existence, we must first be willing to engage each other in serious conversation and begin building a consensus about the nature and possibility of real community.

If Jesus was right when He remarked, "to whom much is given, from him much will be required," (Luke 12:48, NKJV) then it is up to us to make our world a better community by initiating conversations to break down barriers that divide us, and build upon commonalities that bind us together. It was suggested by John F. Kennedy that our success or failure ... will be measured by the answers to four questions—were we truly men of courage ... judgment ... integrity ... dedication?10 I believe a fifth question, certainly regarding authentic community, should be: are we willing to engage each other in meaningful conversation? Let the discourse begin.

—Jarvis

Reflect ...
What is God saying to me?

Respond ...
In response to the devotional, how can I reflect Jesus in my actions?

This week I will ...

-
-
-

How is the Holy Spirit leading me to pray?

Week Fifty

IMPOSSIBLE IS NOTHING

"How will this be," Mary asked the angel, "since I am a virgin?" The angel answered, "The Holy Spirit will overshadow you ... So the holy one to be born will be called the Son of God. Even Elizabeth your relative is going to have a child in her old age, and she who was said to be barren is in her sixth month. For nothing is impossible with God."
—Luke 1:34–37

In 2004 Sports Illustrated published an Adidas advertisement featuring Laila Ali, daughter of world heavyweight boxing champion Muhammed Ali, that read in part, "Impossible is not a fact. It's an opinion ... Impossible is potential. Impossible is temporary. Impossible is nothing."[11] Both daughter and father had had to face seemingly impossible challenges in their lives to reach the success they both ultimately achieved. They were both overcomers who embodied the tag line in the ad: impossible is nothing.

Mary and her cousin, Elizabeth, also faced seemingly impossible challenges. Mary was a virgin; Elizabeth was barren. Yet both would miraculously give birth: Mary, to Him who would be called the Son of God; Elizabeth, to John, who would prepare the way for the ministry of Mary's son.

Although the angel who delivered the message to Mary said it differently than it appeared in the Adidas ad, there must have been a need for additional reassurance, because the angel declared, "Nothing is impossible with God." In other words, with God all things are possible; or, with God, impossible is nothing.

The biblical record is clear. With God, impossible really is nothing. With God, there is no impossible, because our God reigns supreme. He can do anything but fail. And He does all things well. Just ask Mary and Elizabeth—is anything too hard for God?

—**Jarvis**

Reflect ...
What is God saying to me?

Respond ...
In response to the devotional, how can I reflect Jesus in my actions?

This week I will ...

-
-
-

How is the Holy Spirit leading me to pray?

Week Fifty-One

DO YOU SEE DIVINITY?

But the boat was now in the middle of the sea, tossed by the waves ... Now in the fourth watch ... Jesus went to them, walking on the sea. And when the disciples saw Him ... they were troubled, saying, "It is a ghost!" ... But immediately Jesus spoke to them, saying, "Be of good cheer! It is I; do not be afraid."
—Matthew 14:24–27

When you look in the mirror, what do you see? When you look at your family, what do you see? What do you see when you look at the world around you? Do you see divinity?

Matthew records that the disciples, following Jesus's instructions, were together on a boat headed to the other side of the sea. Late that night, they were caught in a storm, and as Jesus approached them walking on the water, they thought He was a ghost. Imagine that. The closest followers of Jesus, in a time of great need, are encountered by the One who can calm troubled waters, and they don't even recognize Him.

I've always said that the failure to recognize divinity in our presence is the root of all ' isms'—racism, sexism, and any other ism imaginable. Our worldview, as well as our treatment of others, may very well be associated with our ability (or inability) to recognize the presence of divinity. If something or someone can be reduced to that which has no connection with divinity, much less humanity, the conditions are right for calamity to occur.

But failure to recognize divinity doesn't mean it isn't there. Jesus was present that late stormy night, and He is present now. He knows who, what, and where you are, and He'll walk on water through a storm to get to you. Will you recognize Him?

—**Jarvis**

Reflect ...
What is God saying to me?

Respond ...
In response to the devotional, how can I reflect Jesus in my actions?

This week I will ...

-
-
-

How is the Holy Spirit leading me to pray?

Week Fifty-Two

GRACE AND PEACE

And the government shall be upon his shoulder: and his name shall be called Wonderful, Counselor, The mighty God, The everlasting Father, the Prince of Peace.
—Isaiah 9:6

The Apostle Paul often used the salutation, "grace and peace." I have borrowed that custom and rarely send any kind of correspondence without some reference to grace and/or peace. The words just seem to fit who I am.

From the beginning of my ministry, my favorite blessing was and continues to be the one given to Moses for the children of Israel: "The Lord bless you and keep you; the Lord make His face shine upon you, and be gracious to you; the Lord lift up His countenance upon you, and give you peace." (Numbers 6:24-26, NKJV) There is something significant to me, and hopefully to you, about offering a blessing—especially one for grace and peace.

The prophet Isaiah also had an interest in the blessings of peace. Having grown up in a world that knew only war, he longed for peace, and he predicted a time when peace and righteousness would be the standard. This era would be ushered in by a Messiah, "and the government would be upon his shoulder, and He would be called … the Prince of Peace."

When I look upon the world as it exists today, I see a great need for peace. Actually, I see a need for the Prince of Peace, because like Isaiah, I know that there is no peace for us, until the Prince of Peace reigns within us. And also like Isaiah, I know that God will keep in perfect peace those whose minds are stayed on Him. (Isaiah 26:3, NKJV)

Grace and peace to you …

—Jarvis

Reflect ...
What is God saying to me?

Respond ...
In response to the devotional, how can I reflect Jesus in my actions?

This week I will ...

-
-
-

How is the Holy Spirit leading me to pray?

Acknowledgments

There are many people who contributed to the success of this project with their prayers, their words of encouragement, and their belief in me and in the God we serve. You know who you are ... and to you I am eternally grateful.

To my wife, Monica, whose loving support sustained and empowered me throughout this incredible journey: "Thanks, I love you, Boo!"

Thank you also to my children, Omari, Matthew, and Skyler, for always inspiring me to be the greatest dad possible.

Additionally, I owe a huge amount of gratitude to my homegrown team of advisors, editors, and supporters. Thank you to Mom and Dad (James and Etta Bailey), for always having my back, and to Kathy Smith, Aunt Florence Bailey, and Aunt Marguerite Young, for your gentle and meaningful review of the manuscript. You all are awesome.

Finally, I want to thank all those who took the time to read this book and engage in devotional time with God. It was my prayer from the beginning that something gleaned from this book would have a positive impact on peoples' lives. And thanks also for your contribution toward making life better for others through the "Greatest Commandment Campaign."

Grace and Peace,
Jarvis

NOTES

Week One—A Word of Encouragement
Text: Romans 8: 38-39 (NKJV)

Week Two—Man Up!
Text: Joshua 24:15 (KJV)

Week Three—Real Security
   Text: Psalm 20:7 (ESV)

Week Four—Be King for a Day (A Tribute to Martin Luther King, Jr.)
   Text: Deuteronomy 4:9
1Haile Selassie, Selected Speeches of His Imperial Majesty Haile Selassie I 1918–1967. Addis Ababa, Ethiopia: The Imperial Ethiopian Ministry of Information Publications and Foreign Languages Press Department, 1967. http://www.himchurch.org/Recommended_Reading/Selected_Speeches/Haile_Selassie_I-Selected_Speeches-Chapter_V-19631006.html

Week Five—You Can Run, But You Can't Hide
   Text: Proverbs 15:3 (NKJV)

Week Six—Who Knows?
Text: Esther 4:14 (NKJV)
2Leonard Sweet. Summoned to Lead. Grand Rapids, MI: Zondervan, 2004.

Week Seven—I Surrender All
   Text: Luke 18:22 (NKJV)

Week Eight—Thirty Seconds to Fame
   Text: Psalms 90:12 (NKJV)

Week Nine—It's How You Finish

Text: Jude 24 (NKJV)

Week Ten—Coffee-Bean Women
    Text: Numbers 27:1–4 (NKJV)

Week Eleven—What's in a Name?
    Text: Genesis 22:14 (NKJV)

Week Twelve—God Willing
    Text: James 4:13–15 (ESV)

Week Thirteen—Finish the Race
    Text: 2 Timothy 4:7–8 (NKJV)

Week Fourteen—More Than Enough
    Text: 2 Corinthians 12:9 (NIV)

Week Fifteen—A Work in Progress
    Text: Philippians 1:6 (NKJV)

Week Sixteen—Unity Is Power
    Text: Genesis 11:6 (ESV)
    [3]Evan Carmichael. "Motivation and Strategies for Entrepreneurs." http://www.evancarmichael.com.

Week Seventeen—Pray for Peace
    Text: Jeremiah 29:7 (NKJV)
    [4]Franklin Roosevelt, Russell Buhite, David Levy, FDR's Fireside Chats (Oklahoma: University of Oklahoma Press, 1992), 162.

Week Eighteen—A Different Way
    Text: Matthew 2:12 (NKJV)

Week Nineteen—My Inheritance
    Text: 2 Timothy 1:5 (NIV)

Week Twenty—Chickens Can't Fly
    Text: Isaiah 40:31 (NLT)

Week Twenty-One—The Old Landmark
    Text: 2 Kings 23:3 (NKJV)

Week Twenty-Two—Meritorious Service
    Text: Job 13:15 (NKJV)
5Civilla Martin, lyrics, and Walter Martin, music, "God Will Take Care of You."   http://www.cyberhymnal.org/htm/g/w/gwiltake.htm.

Week Twenty-Three—A Sure Foundation
    Text: Luke 6:47–48 (NKJV)

Week Twenty-Four—Those Crazy Christians
    Text: 1 Corinthians 1:23 (NIV)

Week Twenty-Five—Authentic Manhood
    Text: 1 Kings 2:2–3 (NKJV)

Week Twenty-Six—It Ain't Always About Us
    Text: Genesis 12:1–2

Week Twenty-Seven—Teach Us to Pray
    Text: Luke 11:1 (ESV)

Week Twenty-Eight—The Real World
    Text: Matthew 11:28 (NLT)

Week Twenty-Nine—Ready for Community?
    Text: Philippians 2:3 (NKJV)

Week Thirty—Beginning at the End
    Text: 2 Corinthians 5:17 (NKJV)

Week Thirty-One – By Our Love
    Text: John 13:35 (ESV)

Week Thirty-Two—It's Your Availability
    Text: 2 Kings 5:2–4 (NKJV)

Week Thirty-Three—Do It!
    Text: 1 Chronicles 4:10 (NKJV)

Week Thirty-Four—Amazing Faith
    Text: Mark 2:5 (NIV)

Week Thirty-Five—Cash versus Character
    Text: 1 Timothy 6:11 (NIV)

Week Thirty-Six—Where's the Fruit?
    Text: John 15:5 (NLT)

Week Thirty-Seven—Hard Work
    Text: 2 Thessalonians 3:10 (NLT)

Week Thirty-Eight—The Children Are Our Future
    Text: Mark 10:14 (NKJV)

6Linda Creed, lyrics, and Michael Masser, music, "Greatest Love of All," performed by George Benson (The Greatest, soundtrack, 1977).

Week Thirty-Nine—Good Examples
    Text: Thessalonians 1:2–3 (NKJV)

    7Douglas Mallock, "Be the Best." http://joyfulministry.com/bebestt.htm.

Week Forty—Keep the Faith, Baby
    Text: Luke 22:32 (NKJV)

Week Forty-One—A New Thing?
    Text: Hebrews 13:8 (KJV)
8Thomas Chisholm, lyrics, and William Runyan, music, "Great Is Thy Faithfulness." Carol Stream, IL: Hope Publishing Company, 1923. http://www.cyberhymnal.org/htm/g/i/gisthyf.htm.

Week Forty-Two—I Pray For You
    Text: James 5:16 (NLT)

Week Forty-Three—Come
    Text: Revelation 22:17 (NKJV)

Week Forty-Four—The Secret of Success
    Text: Matthew 25:21(NKJV)

Week Forty-Five—A Lesson in Giving
    Text: Luke 21:1–4 (MSG)

Week Forty-Six—The Right Question
    Text: Matthew 16:13–15 (NIV)
9David Guzik, The Blue Letter Bible. http://www.blueletterbible.org/cgi-bin/comm_read.pl?book=Mat&chapter=16&verse=15&Comm=Comm%2Fdavid_guzik%2Fsg%2FMat_16.html%230%26*David+Guzik%26&Select.x=25&Select.y=4.

Week Forty-Seven—Remember Who You Are
    Text: 1 Peter 2:9 (NLT)

Week Forty-Eight—Give Thanks
    Text: 1 Thessalonians 5:16–18 (NKJV)

Week Forty-Nine—Moral Discourse
    Text: Proverbs 27:17 (NIV)
    10JFKLibrary.org. Reference Desk.
    http://www.jfklibrary.org/Historical+Resources/Archives/Reference+Desk/Speeches/JFK/.

Week Fifty—Impossible Is Nothing
    Text: Luke 1:34–37 (MSG)
11Laila Ali, http://davidadewumi.com/2008/05/06/greatest-ad-campaign-ever-impossible-is-nothing/.

Week Fifty-One—Do You See Divinity?
    Text: Matthew 14:24–27 (NKJV)

Week Fifty-Two—Grace and Peace
    Text: Isaiah 9:6 (KJV)